Jesus Christ did not intend for His church to be run only by experts, by specialists, by professional consultants.

He knew that His church would be made up of reasonably informed lay people who would do their best to carry on a loving and effective ministry.

That's why this book was written—to provide Sunday school teachers and superintendents with a reasonable amount of sound educational theory, in language they can understand, so they will be equipped with the tools they need for one important ministry of the church: to help children learn.

How Children Learn

Dr. Glenn Heck
Marshall Shelley

David C. Cook Publishing Co.
ELGIN, ILLINOIS—WESTON, ONTARIO

18357

© 1979 David C. Cook Publishing Co.

All rights reserved. Except for brief excerpts for review purposes, no part of this book may be reproduced or used in any form without written permission from the publisher.

Scripture quotations, except where otherwise noted, are taken from the New International Version.

Designer: Rich Nickel
Printed in the United States of America

Library of Congress Catalog Number: 78-67661
ISBN: 0-89191-161-8

First Printing, November 1979
Second Printing, September 1980

CONTENTS

Preface 7

1 Up the Mountain 9
   The Race Is Not to the Swift

2 Planning the Ascent 17
   Can We Get There from Here?

3 One Step at a Time 29
   Informing

4 Don't Just Sit There 37
   Doing

5 A Reason to Go On 45
   Encouraging

6 The View from Here 53
   Assessing

7 Putting It All Together 59
   Summary and Conclusions

PREFACE

How do children learn? It's an important process to understand. But in Christian education, a prior question must be asked: what should children learn?

The purpose of Christian education is summed up in Scripture. "Train a child in the way he should go, and when he is old he will not turn from it" (Prov. 22:6). And Jesus said, "Let the little children come to me, and do not hinder them, for the kingdom of heaven belongs to such as these" (Mt. 19:14). Thus, the task of a child's Christian education is to train him in the ways of God and to introduce him to Jesus.

If children are taught to love God, to follow His commandments, and to experience a personal friendship with Jesus Christ, then truly Christian education will have taken place.

This life-changing spiritual growth process has three elements: knowing, doing, and being.

Christian education starts with knowing. "*Know* that the Lord is God. It is he who made us, and we are his; we are his people, the sheep of his pasture" (Ps. 100:3). In Ephesians 1:18, Paul prays that the people "may *know* the hope to which he has called you, the riches of his glorious inheritance in the saints."

Mere knowing, however, is not enough. This knowledge requires action. In the Old Testament, God tells His people several times to "observe to do." In the New Testament, Jesus makes clear that hearing must be accompanied by doing. Or as James says, "I will show you my faith by what I do" (Jas. 2:18).

The final goal of Christian maturity is more than knowing and more than doing. It's being. That means a faith that becomes a personal characteristic. The Bible tells us to "*be* perfect" and to "*be* holy." It also means a relationship. " 'The time is coming,' declares the Lord, 'when I will make a new covenant with the house of Israel. . . . I will be their God, and they will *be* my people' " (Jer. 33:31-33).

Knowing, doing, and being are all necessary steps in a person's spiritual development. Knowing and doing lead to being. The function of Christian education is to help people clearly know, and effectively do, so that they can truly be.

This book explains how the church can aid that development.

UP THE MOUNTAIN
The Race Is Not to the Swift

My friend and chief adversary in high school was a small, shy girl with dark hair and almond eyes. Kristi made up for her size by intense study, and her test scores almost always set the standard for the rest of the class. Since I was usually the closest also-ran, we constantly monitored each other's progress. After 2½ years of literal head-to-head competition, we were tied with A-plus averages. Then a gym teacher gave Kristi a B, largely because she wasn't as good in track as her longer, leaner classmates. I won the valedictorian honors by a fraction of a percentage, but I remember thinking (though I wouldn't have admitted it) that somehow it wasn't quite right.

Marshall Shelley

HOW CHILDREN LEARN

1

Crack! The starter's pistol fires and the runners are off, straining to take the early lead. There may be dozens, or hundreds, or thousands of runners, depending on the location and the event. But each person runs alone. The object is to pass everyone else.

"Don't look back," the coaches have warned. "Someone may be gaining on you."

It's the education race, and it begins in the earliest years of school. Every student is like a sprinter, running in his own lane, trying to reach the finish line. Some fall behind, but that's natural—someone has to. It's part of the sport.

Brighter students set the pace, and all the spectators focus their attention on them. Runners who falter fall further and further behind, but no one really notices. Eventually they usually either drop out of the race or else finish well behind the winner, virtually ignored.

Up the Mountain

We have outgrown the days of dunce caps, hickory switches, and moving prize students to the head of the class. We have stopped physical punishment and ridicule for failure to learn, but until very recently, schools still approached learning as a competitive process. Grades were based on the curve—only a few students could earn the coveted A. The object of the education game was to improve in the class ranking, and the only way to advance was at the expense of someone else.

In the past few years, some educators began wondering if this was the best way of learning. Specifically, Dr. Benjamin Bloom, professor of education at the University of Chicago, became curious about the differences in school achievement between students. Why do some finish the race faster than others? Was it heredity? Home environment? Luck? Or the Lord?

In an attempt to explain individual differences and to find ways, if possible, to help students who were falling behind, Bloom began extensive observation, research, and experimentation. In 1976, his book *Human Characteristics and School Learning* was published and revealed what he discovered.

It shook the secular educational world. Its implications still haven't been fully realized, but the changes that it has already helped bring about in curriculum and teaching technique have been profound.

And, ironically, his basic idea is what Christians have believed for years and what Christian education is based on—that virtually anyone can learn, given the right learning environment.

Bloom's research disproved the idea that some people are *good* learners and others are *poor* learners. He discovered that with appropriate conditions of learning "what any person in the world can learn, almost all persons can learn." He qualified that a bit by allowing for 2 or 3 percent of the

HOW CHILDREN LEARN

students to be in the exceptional category—geniuses at one end and those with learning disabilities at the other. But everyone else had almost equal potential.

It was a radical, powerful statement. If 95 percent of the students can learn anything that anyone else has learned, we have no excuse for not providing everyone with that kind of education. Indeed, thirty-three states in the United States have passed laws or taken steps to require not just equal opportunity for education, but also equal output. Everyone must meet certain levels of competency, or as Bloom called it, "mastery."

What was Bloom's approach? How was he able to get 95 percent success? The first key was adjusting the current model of education.

Instead of education being a race, Bloom found it more effective when seen as a group effort—something like a team of mountain climbers, roped together, straining for the summit. Yes, there's still competition, but it's group competition—the group against the mountain.

The group cannot proceed unless the first person is making progress. And the group hasn't completed its task until the last person on the line has reached the top. If anyone falls or meets an obstacle, the rest of the group don't rush past him—they help him up and over the snag. It may take a bit longer and require more effort, but everyone arrives.

This has been essentially the approach of Sunday school ever since 1780, when founder Robert Raikes used the more advanced pupils as "monitors" to help teach the others. While public schools were concentrating on grade-point averages, streaming practices, and generally making education a race, the church was quietly helping everyone along. Slowly, to be sure—often the pace was no more than a crawl. And sometimes the group wandered without the direction clearly in mind. But the group was moving, and it was helping everyone toward the peak.

Up the Mountain

Christians have always wanted to bring *all* to a knowledge of and commitment to Jesus Christ. Spiritual growth isn't every man for himself. Jesus said, "If anyone wants to be first, he must be the very last, and the servant of all" (Mk. 9:35).

Paul said, "Build each other up. . . . Warn those who are idle, encourage the timid, help the weak, be patient with everyone" (I Thess. 5:11-14).

It is comforting to have a mountain climber's rope around your waist to catch you when you fall and to help you over the difficult spots. But it is also a responsibility to hold the rope for others and assist them over the terrain you've just covered.

Since Christians already agree with the basic idea behind Dr. Bloom's work, it is helpful to study his techniques for actually putting this approach to use. Not only will it show us how children learn, but also how teachers and parents can help the learning happen, whether in a public school classroom, church school, or Sunday school class.

This model is not the final word on Christian education. But it is a way of visualizing how learning happens. When we can see its various parts, it allows us to evaluate our students' learning, anticipate problems, and remedy the weaknesses.

To illustrate each of the steps in the process, imagine a coach teaching someone how to serve a tennis ball.

The first step is for both the coach and the student to know what the goal is—a fluid, powerful, effective serve. And then the coach must discover how much the student already knows. He will observe the student serving a number of times, noting the way the student stands, holds his racquet, swings, and hits the ball. The coach makes mental note of the aspects that must be worked on. All of this is the *planning* stage.

Then the coach begins his teaching by *informing* the

HOW CHILDREN LEARN

student of what he needs to learn. Perhaps he is not tossing the ball high enough. Perhaps the swing is jerky. Perhaps he isn't shifting his weight correctly. The coach begins directing the student by working on one thing at a time.

The student must respond by *doing*—trying to apply the coach's directions. Sometimes it must be practiced over and over.

As the student does it right, the coach will be *encouraging* him by verbal comments, a smile, or a nod. Perhaps the most encouragement, however, comes as the student sees his own progress toward the goal and his serve improves.

Finally, at various points in the learning process, the coach will check to see what the student has accomplished, perhaps watching the student in a tournament to see how effective the serve actually is. This is called the *assessing* stage and gives both coach and student an idea of how much progress has been made and how much still must be done.

Thus, these are the components of how children learn—planning, informing, doing, encouraging, assessing. In the following chapters, each component will be described in greater depth to show how it might help the educational process in the church, home, and Sunday school.

To return to the mountain-climbing analogy, these components won't guarantee that we'll all reach the top, but they will allow more members of our expedition to near the summit than any other technique.

Up the Mountain

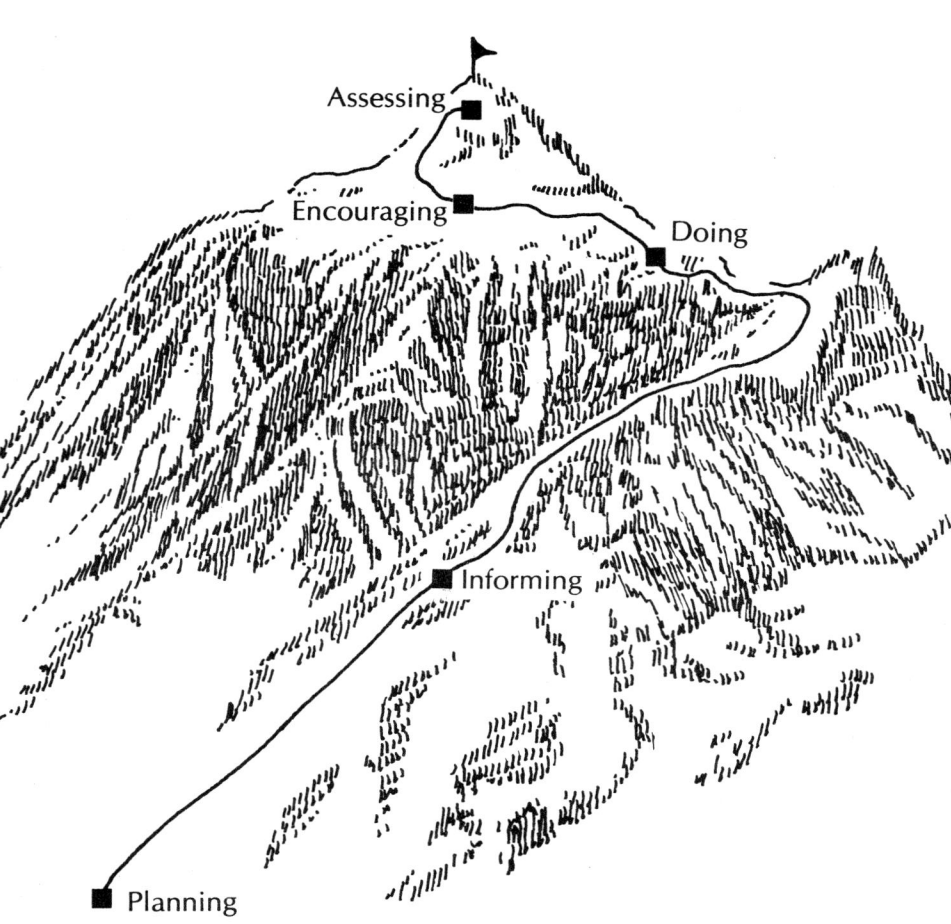

THE GROWTH PROCESS

PLANNING THE ASCENT
Can We Get There from Here?

"Cheshire-Puss," she began, rather timidly. . . . "Would you tell me, please, which way I ought to go from here?"

"That depends a good deal on where you want to get to," said the Cat.

"I don't much care where–" said Alice.

"Then it doesn't matter which way you go," said the Cat.

Lewis Carroll
Alice's Adventures in Wonderland

2

Before any expedition can begin its assault on the summit, someone must decide three things:
- where the group will start.
- which mountain they will climb.
- what equipment is necessary.

The same three things must also be known before life-changing learning can take place. Once these have been agreed upon, the climb becomes much easier.

THE STARTING POINT

Both the leader and his climbers must agree where they will start. Otherwise, they may never find one another to begin.

One Sunday school teacher was having a miserable time with his class of rowdy fifth-grade boys. They weren't interested in the lessons, and their boredom translated into chaos.

Planning the Ascent

"We already know all this stuff," they said. "Why do we have to hear the same old Bible story again?"

"You're right," said the teacher. "If you already know it, we don't need to cover it again. But I want to make sure you *know* it, not just know *about* it. Would you be willing to take a quiz on it next week?"

"Sure."

The next week the lesson was on Solomon. The teacher gave a ten-question quiz—not obscure questions, but a legitimate review of the key lessons to be learned from Solomon's life. What did God give Solomon? What was the main project he worked on during his life? What was his worst sin? What happened because of it? And so on.

To the students' amazement, no one got more than three answers right! They thought they knew the story, but when it came down to it, they really didn't. The class worked hard for the rest of the lessons on Solomon. And at the end, the teacher gave them the same quiz again, and everyone got all the answers right. They had mastered the material; they had conquered the peak. But they wouldn't have if they hadn't discovered their starting point.

Sometimes children need to be convinced of what they don't know. Then, when they see what needs to be learned, they're usually eager to do it. The important thing is that both teacher and students discover what they know already and begin building from there.

Another way to do this is by going over the table of contents in the Sunday school material and asking the students what they think is most important to study this quarter. An entire session could be spent merely discussing what's most important, least important, most interesting, least interesting, and why. If something is both important and interesting to the students, they will be motivated to learn it. And this is where teaching should begin.

If children are already further up the mountain than we

HOW CHILDREN LEARN

expect them to be, for goodness sakes don't make them come back down to start at the bottom again! But sometimes students, such as the fifth-grade boys mentioned earlier, don't have an accurate idea of where they really are. Their present location needs to be determined.

The first job of the teacher is to find out where most of the class is, round them up, and point out to them the mountaintop.

WHICH MOUNTAIN?

The ultimate goal of Christian education is to raise people to be mature followers of Jesus Christ. "Be perfect, therefore, as your heavenly Father is perfect," said Jesus (Mt. 5: 48). That's a tall order, certainly a higher mountain than anyone could handle in a single step. We need to work toward it by conquering the lower ranges first.

Learning is most effective if the teacher can identify what the students should learn and how they will know when they have mastered it. Most of the better printed curriculums will give you some indicators.

Begin each new unit by identifying these things. You may want to share your list with the students, especially if they are fifth grade or above. Show them the peak they're climbing for, and where they'll be camping along the way. It's easier to learn when you know not only what you don't know, but what you're trying for.

Things on your list will generally fall into these categories:
- Content.
- Bible study skills.
- Social awareness.
- Spiritual development.

Now look at what you might expect a young person to

Planning the Ascent

master in each of these four areas.

Content. This is factual knowledge, which, for example, might include knowing such things as the general geographic pattern of Paul's missionary journeys. Students might demonstrate they've learned the material by mapping Paul's travels and identifying the key places where he stayed.

Remember, however, that head knowledge isn't the only thing that matters. Other skills are equally important in growing toward maturity.

Bible study skills. Another goal of the Sunday school teacher is to train young people to study God's Word for themselves, especially as they grow into adolescence. One of the most important goals of teaching is to help students "learn to learn."

They might demonstrate this skill by sharing aloud some techniques for inductive Bible study and showing some written work they've done on a particular Bible book.

They should also be familiar with other Bible study aids—concordances, maps, Bible dictionaries, Bible encyclopedias. Fourth, fifth, and sixth grades are a prime time to introduce these resources. That is the age when students are learning all about the world. Many are eager to sit down with a book and discover facts that most people don't know—they enjoy becoming an expert in some particular area. (Ever heard a ten-year-old spout obscure facts about dinosaurs?) Resources such as *The Family Bible Encyclopedia* (Cook) can introduce them to the world of Bible times and can explain concepts in language they can understand. We need to help students feel at home in the biblical world.

Social awareness. People of all ages need to learn to interact comfortably with people of their own age, people older and younger, and people from different backgrounds. They must learn to be aware of the needs of other people and help meet them.

HOW CHILDREN LEARN

In the classroom, part of this process can be observed in class discussion, through roleplay, and working in groups.

Spiritual development. Being a mature follower of Jesus Christ means more than hearing and knowing. A recurring phrase in the Bible is "observe to do"—that means acting, participating, doing. Learning to live the Christian faith is perhaps the most important goal of Christian education.

It may be impossible for teachers to know when students have mastered spiritual lessons, but the young people will give verbal and life-action clues.

Teachers should pray daily that their students will apply the lessons they have studied to their lives.

Teachers should also make certain they have clearly presented how biblical principles should be lived. Spiritual progress may be slowed if the teachers don't share how students should respond to what they've learned.

Here's an example of a response idea a junior high teacher might give: "Today we emphasized the importance of respecting parents. Easier said than done. So I have an idea how you could discover how well you live this principle. This week, every time you fail to respect your parents, whether in attitude or action, jot it down on a slip of paper. And each time you do respect them, jot that down, too. Next week we'll see how many of each we have."

Spiritual learning is seen in ability to analyze situations, apply biblical principles, and find creative solutions.

WHAT EQUIPMENT DO WE NEED?

Before setting out on a strenuous climb, a good leader will make sure all the climbers have the proper equipment. If someone is without shoes, he ought to be given a pair before the group begins the ascent. Otherwise that person will

Planning the Ascent

never make it, and it will cause frustration and problems for everyone else.

Dr. Benjamin Bloom's research indicated that 95 percent of all students could master a given body of material if three conditions were met:
- if they entered the course adequately prepared.
- if they were well motivated.
- if the instruction was appropriate to the learner.

Let's look at these one at a time.

Adequate preparation. Naturally the amount of preparation depends on the toughness of the hill you're going to climb. A stroll up a grassy hill might not even demand shoes. But serious rock climbing requires ropes, pitons, a hammer, and some technical know-how.

Children in preschool classes would have few requirements. But in high school classes, students should know how to read, how to interact in small peer groups, and it's helpful, though not mandatory, that they have some knowledge about Christ's life and what it means to be a Christian.

What if a person doesn't have the necessary prerequisites? Or what if he falls behind the others and doesn't grasp some of the necessary background early in the course?

Bloom discovered an amazing thing. With outside help, almost all students could catch up. This tutoring could be done by the teacher, by the parents, by another student in the class, or by an adult "pal."

Initially, these students might require five times as much time to learn the same concepts as the rest of the class. But Bloom discovered that they could learn equally complex and abstract ideas as anyone else—it just took longer. And as these students "learned to learn," they began needing less and less time to catch on until they were caught up and keeping pace with everyone else.

Motivation. The most powerful motivation is seeing personal progress. When people are given the necessary extra

HOW CHILDREN LEARN

time and attention, they will make progress. It may be slow, but when they see it, it becomes an incentive for further work.

The teacher is also a key instrument in motivating students. The teacher's attitude toward the material is contagious—if he's bored, the students will be also; if he continually looks for fresh ideas that even he hasn't seen before, then the students will tend to do the same.

The goal should be to motivate all the students. Naturally, not many teachers reach that goal. Don't be disappointed if you don't—in some cases you will be struggling with attitudes that have been developing for years.

Be patient and pray daily for each student. It's much harder to lose patience and temper with someone when you've prayed for that person that day.

Get to know each student and the things he likes. At every opportunity incorporate those elements into your teaching.

Appropriate instruction. Both the choice of mountains to be climbed and the routes taken to get to the top must be selected with the abilities of the students taken into account. Beginning hikers are in no shape to tackle Mount McKinley. The same is true of children's learning processes. As their minds and bodies mature, they're ready for more difficult subjects. But they have to learn the basics first.

For preschool children, for instance, the goals should be simple—perhaps such things as:
- God is great, powerful, and can be trusted.
- Jesus is our loving friend.
- God created the world for us to enjoy, and He expects us to take care of it.
- The church is God's family.

If preschoolers can learn these things and experience the warmth and love associated with those ideas, they will be well on their way up the mountain.

Teachers also need to be aware of the different stages

Planning the Ascent

young people pass through, because those stages affect the student's learning ability. Teaching must be adapted to the student's ability to learn.

Research is showing, for example, that giving too much additional information in the early teen years might actually harm the emerging adolescent's ability to grow later on.

Why? Because in perhaps 85 percent of all people between the ages of twelve and fourteen, the brain virtually ceases to grow, which results in a learning plateau. This helps explain the difficulty of teaching junior high students.

We mentioned earlier that fourth through sixth graders are eager to learn. That's because their minds are in a growing period. They are ready to absorb concrete knowledge. After the plateau through, roughly, seventh and eighth grades, students are better able to learn new things again.

The time between the concrete knowledge growth spurt and the emerging abstract knowledge growth spurt is the ideal time to review what the students know and help them begin practicing it. Junior high years are a good time to begin giving students an opportunity to work in the church—serving perhaps in the nursery or singing in choirs.

After this period of settling in, the young person begins, between the ages of fourteen and sixteen, the last great brain growth he will experience. There is renewed interest in learning new things. This is the time to cover some difficult subjects that the students have not yet studied—for example, theology, great debated issues of Christianity, church history, ethical questions. Students are finally ready to begin thinking abstractly.

Interestingly, educators considering the brain growth patterns are beginning to think that one reason many young people drop out of high school in the years of their greatest brain growth is because they were burned out in junior high. They were overloaded with complex input during the years when their minds should have been resting. They blew a

HOW CHILDREN LEARN

circuit! For these people, their teaching in junior high forced them to move ahead of their maturation level. They just gave up. A year or two later they weren't able to use their brain capacity as effectively. Their cognitive growth came to a screeching and tragic halt.

It's like trying to sprint up a mountain. It can't be done. Climbers have to pace themselves, sometimes stopping for rest before renewing the assault. Junior highers also need time to consolidate what they know, to begin developing social skills, and to rest from an overload of serious content work.

(For more information, see "A Neuroscience Basis for Reorganizing Middle Grades Education" by Herman T. Epstein and Conrad R. Toepfer, Jr., in the May, 1978, issue of *Educational Leadership*.)

The point is, know what your students are capable of, stretch them, but don't force them beyond their capacities. That can be dangerous. Learning is a continuing process. Education doesn't stop after high school or even college. A person doesn't need to learn everything as a child. Members of God's family, especially, are involved in lifelong learning. Take it at a sensible pace.

Take a look at the curriculum materials you use. They should be your best resource in helping you plan lessons appropriate to your students' levels of development. But make sure the materials are doing their job. Compare them with what you know about your students and what you've learned about the learning process so far in this book.

Here are some points to check:
- Do the lessons cover content that is appropriate to the age level? Is it interesting and important to the students?
- Are the lessons helping students to think on their own? Some studies allow students to sit through the hour without ever thinking or studying for themselves.

Planning the Ascent

- Do the lessons provide opportunities for students to learn how to interact with each other in structured and unstructured situations? Learning to work with other people is crucial.
- Do the studies touch real life? Are the spiritual lessons taught more than just head knowledge? Curriculum should help make clear how biblical principles affect the students' lives.

Demand a lot from the materials you use. God has assigned you a difficult task—guiding the learning process. Don't use less than the best help available to get the job done.

ONE STEP AT A TIME
Informing

My father was a sturdy, methodical German. Every morning and every evening he gathered the family for twenty minutes of Bible reading and ten minutes of prayer. Everyone, whether age four or forty, took his turn reading. And each year we managed to read the entire Bible.

When I was in eighth grade, we were reading James 4 one evening, and suddenly a verse leaped out at me—"To him that knoweth to do good, and doeth it not, to him it is sin."

Uh-oh, *I thought. I'm in trouble. I know it all! I had read the Bible cover to cover ten times, and I knew there wasn't a chance in the world of obeying it all before Christmas. So I came to the conclusion that only a fourteen-year-old would make: my only hope was to stop reading it.*

Glenn Heck

HOW CHILDREN LEARN

3

The Glenn-Heck-at-fourteen response wasn't entirely wrong. Too much information had been given without enough explanation of what should be done with it. No attempt was made to determine what was important to begin working on right away and what could wait for a while.

A group of mountain climbers cannot simply be told "Go climb Mount Everest" and be expected to leap to the top. They need to know which route they are taking and how far they can expect to get in one day. They need to know where the campsites are along the way.

It's easy to become discouraged if a person just looks at the massiveness of the mountain and the miles he must go and the rough terrain he must cover before he reaches the summit. But if he concentrates only on reaching the spot where he planned to stop for the night, the job seems more manageable.

Knowing more than you know what to do with can be frustrating, yet there is a place for knowledge for knowl-

One Step at a Time

edge's sake. Father Heck wasn't entirely wrong either. There are two kinds of knowing, and both are valuable in their own way.

First, there's *acquaintance*. That's "knowing about," knowing generally that something exists. Most of us, for example, have some vague idea of what happens underneath the hood of a car—gasoline is mixed with air and burned, which produces the power that makes the wheels turn. Or perhaps a person knows that the story of Jesus is told in the four Gospels.

This kind of knowledge is valuable because it allows us to categorize what we know. We mentally file it away. Then when the occasion arises that we need more specific information, we know where to look. We have a framework; we know how this information fits in with the rest of the world.

The second kind of knowledge is *mastery*. That is knowing something so well that you recognize its importance, how it affects things, and what it demands of you. It's knowing the car engine well enough that when it refuses to start, you know what to do to start it again. It's knowing why the life of Jesus is important, what He taught, and how your life should be different as a result.

Mastery is useful knowledge. It's knowledge in action; learning that makes a difference. Mastery is the goal of Christian education—helping people become effective Christians, obeying the commands of Christ, exhibiting the fruit of the Spirit. It's much more than simply knowing about them.

When working with young people, we need to let them know which kind of knowledge we're after. The Heck family Bible reading was a valuable source of Bible acquaintance. It was too much, however, for a fourteen-year-old boy to master.

In this book, we're primarily concerned with mastery. True Christian education aims to produce mature believers,

HOW CHILDREN LEARN

people who really know what they believe, and why, and how to live it.

Thus, after planning, the next step in the learning process is *informing*—giving bite-sized ideas to be digested. Learning must start with knowing. It's hard enough to do what you know, but it's impossible to do what you don't know. Informing is the step that provides the necessary knowledge, and it has two phases.

WHAT TO MASTER

The first thing the student must be told is what he or she is going to learn. In Sunday school, teachers have fifty-two lessons a year. For most students, it would be impossible to learn fifty-two life-changing lessons every year.

When it comes to mastery, we must choose our battlefields carefully. Work on one thing at a time. Students can become acquainted with different material each week, but the material to be mastered will have to be emphasized again and again. Let the students know what's really important.

One teacher began teaching a group of high school students and discovered they were continually backbiting, criticizing, and gossiping about one another.

"I fought in World War II," he said, "but this was the most vicious bunch of people I'd ever seen!"

He decided that the most important thing the students needed to learn was love, and it should begin with showing some appreciation for one another.

"So I told them that I didn't want them to come to class next week until they had paid someone else in the class a sincere compliment," the teacher explained. "It could be anybody—as long as the person was a fellow student and

One Step at a Time

the compliment was genuine. They all agreed that they could do that much."

The next week the teacher checked on the results. He discussed with the class what kinds of compliments were given and how they could look for the admirable traits in people. Then he gave the next week's assignment—give two sincere compliments. Each week he increased the dosage.

"In six months," he reported, "that group was transformed. The backbiting stopped, the viciousness was gone, and they were actually caring about one another. It wouldn't have happened unless we had spent considerable time on it. A one-Sunday lesson just wasn't enough."

As teachers look over their lessons for the quarter, they should notice the lesson aims. Which ones should be emphasized most? How can the class work on that for several weeks? As a general rule, choose one aim for a month, and let the informing begin there.

One of the real needs of the church is more research on the child's developmental stages and what spiritual lessons should be learned when. Curriculum publishers are working with this problem, and this is one area where seminaries could provide tremendous help. What are the appropriate directions for each age level? More work remains to be done.

HOW TO INFORM

Informing is a bit like telling a lost tourist how to get back to the highway. You start from where he is and give him specific direction from that point. He can only understand one turn at a time.

A good teacher also starts with the present location of the students—using language they understand, illustrations

HOW CHILDREN LEARN

they can relate to, and analogies they're familiar with. Teachers will often need to repeat directions several times until everyone has grasped exactly what is to be done.

A teacher should have a variety of ways of informing—verbal instructions, setting up learning centers, giving examples, or drawing pictures, charts, or graphs. Directions may take the form of models, observations of self or others, or demonstrating something the student is to reproduce in some way. No single way is best. In fact, the greater the variety of instructional materials and methods used, the greater the likelihood that each student will secure the information he needs for his learning.

Good teachers often ask different students to put the assignment in their own words. Often the students who don't understand what the teacher was talking about can understand when it's explained by a fellow student.

Actually most teachers are better than they are brave. That is, their intuitive sense of what is getting across is usually pretty accurate. When teachers get to know their students, the ability to communicate appropriate directions comes naturally. Some teachers are reluctant to try their own teaching ideas for fear they won't work. Be brave! If you think it fits your group, chances are it will.

What's the general structure a class time should have? It varies, of course, depending upon what's being covered and the interests of the students. But generally the following four segments are a good outline to follow.

Life Need. Open the class by showing how the topic for the day relates to the students' everyday world. There are all kinds of creative ways this can be done—pointed discussion questions, reading a clipping from the daily newspaper, a skit, or presenting a problem that needs to be solved. Most printed curriculum guides provide plenty of ideas. The point is to let the students see that what they're studying today is important to them.

One Step at a Time

Bible Learning. After introducing the subject, then we need to see what the Bible says about it, or how people in the Bible dealt with it. Christian education needs to be based on the Word of God. Biblical principles and values are the basis for Christian education.

Bible Application. These biblical principles need to be linked to life and illustrated so that students can understand them. Often this is done by showing how contemporary people are putting the principles to work. Students need to see that Bible truth isn't limited to Bible times. It makes a difference today.

Life Response. This is where the application gets specific and personal. What are you going to do with your new knowledge of the Bible? How can we as a class work on this problem? These are the questions dealt with in the life response. It is here that the teacher needs to be careful that the students are working on what is really important. If students consider their work trivial, they won't stick with it very long.

More on response and doing will be covered in the next chapter as we consider the next step of the learning process—acting on what you know.

As your group of mountain climbers inches its way up the mountain, keep pointing out the direction they should go. That's what informing is. But be sure the landmark you point them to isn't so far off it's out of sight. Focus on the immediate and visible goal. If you don't, the group is much more likely to get lost.

DON'T JUST SIT THERE
Doing

"*Swallow your food before you take another bite!*"
Almost any mother

But be doers of the word, and not hearers only.
James 1:22

HOW CHILDREN LEARN

4

Mountain climbers can study the route to the top all day, but until they actually start moving, they aren't any closer to the summit than before.

In the same way, receiving the right information is the beginning of learning. The ideas, the informing, the directions come first. "I got in trouble because I didn't think first," a child often realizes. The correction process starts with knowing.

But there's more to learning than merely knowing. Simply presenting directions to a student is not likely to produce much lasting effect. The student must participate, either actively or mentally. The student must do something with what he knows.

This is, of course, a biblical concept. God told Joshua to "observe to do" (Josh. 1:7-8, KJV). That phrase also is repeated again and again in the Book of Deuteronomy. Jesus said near the end of the Sermon on the Mount that the wise man was one who both hears the words of Christ and puts them into practice (Mt. 7:24-27).

Don't Just Sit There

A lawyer once approached Jesus and tried to cross-examine Him with some tricky theological questions.

"Teacher," he said. "What must I do to inherit eternal life?"

Jesus responded by making sure the lawyer had the right information. "What is written in the Law?" Christ asked.

The lawyer recited his head knowledge. "Love the Lord your God with all your heart . . . and love your neighbor as yourself."

"You have answered correctly," Jesus replied. "*Do* this and you will live." Christ took the argument to another level by showing that learning isn't just knowing answers—it's doing.

Even then, however, the lawyer didn't get the message. He tried to keep the matter strictly intellectual. "And who is my neighbor?"

A good teacher, Jesus had a variety of ways of informing, so He used a different one—He told a story. It was about a man who was mugged, robbed, and left for dead beside the road. Two respectable men passed by, taking no notice of the battered victim. Then a Samaritan, an outcast, came by and took care of the man.

"Which of these three do you think was a neighbor to the man who fell into the hands of robbers?" Jesus asked, making sure the lawyer understood the story.

"The one who had mercy on him."

"Go and *do* likewise," Jesus concluded.

Several principles of effective teaching are found in this story from Luke 10: 25-37.

First, Jesus found out what the man already knew. He discovered he had the right head knowledge.

Second, when the man showed that he didn't know what to do with that knowledge, Jesus changed His teaching technique, repeated the directions, and gave an example. Some people need directions explained several different ways before they sink in and are understood.

Third, Jesus demanded that the lawyer do something with the knowledge. Christ's information isn't simply to be filed away in the memory. He expects a response—action.

Our teaching should be the same way. Knowing comes before doing. But only when you act on what you know is it going to become part of you. Only when a person starts acting on the biblical commands does he begin to become the person God wants him to be.

The vicious senior high class mentioned in the previous chapter didn't start to change until they began acting on the directions. Merely talking about the problem wasn't the solution. Something had to be *done*. Even though the steps were small—just a single compliment—they were finally starting to move, finally making progress up the mountain.

The same is true even if the educational goal is not a specific behavior but to understand a certain body of material—for instance, the story of Joseph. Younger children can act on the story by performing a play of Joseph's life or by drawing a series of pictures portraying the major events of his life. To do either of those things, the students would have to learn the facts and act on them. Chances of retaining the material are greatly increased.

Older children and adults might want to act on the material in a different way. Doing doesn't have to be overt—sometimes mental activity is just as effective. For instance, with the story of Joseph being thrown into a pit and then sold into slavery by his brothers (Gen. 37), you can pose questions that stretch people's ability to think, that make them say, "I never thought about that before."

Perhaps your line of discussion questions could go something like this:

What was Reuben's (the oldest brother) attitude toward Joseph? What did he do?

Do you think it would have been wiser for Reuben to defy

Don't Just Sit There

his other brothers? Explain. Why or why not?
What else could he have done? What were his options?
Did Reuben's actions show that he trusted God to work everything out, or was he just a coward?
What would you have done?

Questions like these present a twist to the material, an unusual look from a different perspective, from someone other than the main character. These questions are also open-ended; most of them have no "right" answer. Students are able to see Reuben's moral dilemma. They are able to think through the consequences that different actions might have had. This kind of discussion stretches students' ability to think, to reason, and to prepare for similar situations that might face them in the future.

This kind of discussion also exposes students to the way other people reason. More mature moral reasoning comes from exposure to people who operate on higher moral levels. Questions that stretch people's thinking can be some of the most effective ways of stimulating mental action and spiritual growth.

TIME ON TASK

Educational researchers have discovered another important fact about learning that seems painfully obvious to most of us, but which needs to be dealt with more than it is.

They've found that the longer the time spent on a given task the better it's learned. A person who practices the piano five days a week will be a more effective performer than a person who practices one day a week. Increasing the "time on task" increases the learning.

Most people who have difficulty grasping a subject can get it if they increase their time on task. Bloom discovered

HOW CHILDREN LEARN

that "the slowest 10 percent of students may need about five to six times as much rehearsal, practice, or participation in the learning activity as the most rapid 10 percent of students" (*Human Characteristics and School Learning,* p. 122).

Increasing the time on task may mean spending more time informing, more time doing, more time reinforcing, or more time doing all of the above.

Mentally, we give assent to this idea, but we have to admit that most teachers and schools (even Sunday schools) typically function as though all students should learn with approximately the same amount of practice or participation. We don't allow for additional time on task for those who need it.

A fast student may hear a Bible story once and have it for life. A slower student will need to go over the material four, five, seven times before it becomes his.

Some of this repetition could be done during class time with different learning activities that review the material. Some could be done by having a faster student spend some extra time with a slower student reviewing the subject. This would provide an opportunity for the faster student to act on the material as well as providing more time on task for the slower student. For the slowest students, the teacher may want to work through the parents—encouraging them to talk through the content of the lesson with their child during the week.

A good teacher recognizes that the amount of time on task needed will vary from learner to learner. Some students require less overt practice than others. Some students can learn an entire operation (such as having a personal daily Bible study) in a few practice efforts while other learners must practice parts of the operation separately until they gain competence in each one before they put them all together.

Don't Just Sit There

TO DO OR NOT TO DO

One of the most important things the church can do is to identify the distinctive behavior that distinguishes the Christian. For too many years, Christian behavior meant only not smoking, not drinking, not going to movies or roller-skating rinks. Those things may still have a place in Christian behavior, but the church could really help its people if it could help them know what to do, and not just what not to do.

Christian education needs to be able to direct people to *do* the right things, and these actions should be appropriate for each age level. For instance, the following are a few sample ideas.

Preschoolers need to learn that Jesus loves them and that they can show their love back to Him by helping their parents around the house—picking up their dirty clothes, cleaning up their toys, and going to bed without fussing. Even simple faith has practical implications!

First and second graders need to work on getting along with one another, to show kindness even when others do not, to feel sorry when they do wrong, to ask for forgiveness, and to know that God will forgive them.

Third and fourth graders should learn to read the Bible for themselves and accept it as a guide for their behavior.

Fifth and sixth graders can begin practicing a personal devotional time, including Bible reading and prayer—not simply reciting a memorized prayer, but talking to God in their own words.

Junior highers have reached the place where they are aware of what they've learned and are able to pass it on to others. They can begin to practice using their gifts and abilities. Junior high years are a good time to begin giving students opportunities to serve in the church—perhaps helping in the nursery or teaching Bible stories to preschoolers.

HOW CHILDREN LEARN

High school students need to think through the reasons for their behavior and begin to implement Christian ethics in their personal lives even when it's unpopular to do so.

Adults might need to be encouraged to spend more time with their families, or to practice hospitality with neighbors, or to devote half an hour each day to God's service—doing something they wouldn't ordinarily do to help someone else as the occasion arises.

Please don't get hung up by what's not on this list. It could certainly be made a lot longer. Needs of individual groups will indicate what behaviors need to be worked on. The point is that we must identify the kinds of things Christians should do and help one another with the doing part of the learning process.

Our climb up the mountain of Christian maturity isn't going to succeed unless we move—taking one step at a time and grasping the handholds that are within reach.

The mountain won't be leaped in a single bound, but it won't be climbed at all unless we decide to act.

A REASON TO GO ON
Encouraging

My new seventh-grade students were in their seats, waiting silently, a bit fearfully, for their first junior high class to begin. Suddenly we heard footsteps coming down the hall, the sound of heavy, cleated boots.

"Uh-oh," one girl said softly to a friend sitting near her, "Stan is going to be in our class this year." And sure enough, in he walked—a four-foot, eight-inch picture of toughness and cool.

I didn't quite know what to make of Stan, and he didn't know how to take me. So for the first few weeks of school, we just eyed each other. Stan didn't do much work in class, but I didn't want to react until I knew what to do.

One day while giving the class a spelling test, I had

an idea. Stan was a terrible speller, and his handwriting was worse. But spelling was the only subject in which he even made an effort. So after class I asked Stan to see me.

"How many words did you get right on the spelling test today?"

"Two."

"How many did you get right last week?"

"Two."

"How many words do you think you'll get right next week?"

"Two." (At least he was being honest.)

"Stan, I think you're right. Why don't you do me a favor and save yourself some work? Just write down the two you're going to get right."

As far as Stan was concerned, that was the first intelligent thing I'd said all year. He nodded. As he turned to leave, I added, "Hey, Stan, just one other thing. Do you think you could write those two words so I could read them?"

"Oh, yeah. I can do that." And he walked out the door.

When the next week's spelling test was given, Stan sat back and relaxed for the first five words. Then came one he was ready for—a short one. He started scrawling, erasing, and redoing it as I went on down the list. When I got to the seventeenth word, Stan was ready for another try. He worked on it until it was time to grade the papers.

We went over the answers as a class, and as was my custom, I called off the student's names and had them tell me their grades. None wrong was an A, one or two wrong a B, three to five wrong a C, and more than that "not so good."

I could see Stan thinking as I started through the class

A Reason to Go On

list . . . Dennis . . . Carol . . . Mark. Finally I got to him.
"Stan."
"A."

Every head in the room snapped around. Then almost immediately everyone looked back up at me, refusing to believe I'd accept that from Stan. I proceeded down the list . . . Lisa . . . Steve . . . .

After class, Stan came up to my desk. Never before had he approached me on his own. "What grade did you put down in that grade book?" he said softly.

"An A. Isn't that what you told me?"

"Yeah," he said and turned to leave. But he hadn't reached the door before he turned to ask one more question.

"Did you put it in ink?"

I opened the grade book and showed him. He stared at it, transfixed. He'd never seen an A after his name before. He blinked his eyes a few times, and his voice wavered just a bit when he said, "What are you going to tell the other kids?"

"I'm not going to tell them anything. But, Stan, do you think there's any chance that next week you could spell three words right, and neat enough for me to read them?"

"Sure, I could spell three right."

"Do you think that each week you could spell one more word than you did the week before?"

"Oh, yeah. No problem."

Eighteen weeks later, Stan spelled all twenty words right. He never missed a single spelling word for the rest of the year. I should mention, for the sake of honesty, that Stan didn't learn much math or geography or English that year. But he did learn spelling. He was onto a winner.

Glenn Heck

HOW CHILDREN LEARN

5

Mountain climbers get tired. Long treks and difficult terrain often discourage climbers, especially those tackling the tougher slopes for the first time.

One of the most important tasks of the head of the expedition is to keep the group moving. And to do that, he or she will have to keep them encouraged. Without motivation, without reinforcement, the climbers start straggling, obstacles seem bigger, and more people start thinking about giving up the idea of reaching the summit.

In helping children learn, the same is true. If knowledge, attitudes, and learned behaviors are to stick, they need to be reinforced. Students need to be encouraged to stay with it until the learning becomes part of them.

In Sunday school, there are three main sources of encouragement: teachers, parents and other allies, and students themselves. We'll look at each of these one at a time.

TEACHERS

Most of us would agree that Sunday schools should give everyone in the class equal opportunity to learn. In actual practice, however, this rarely happens. Most teachers quite unconsciously direct their teaching at some students and

A Reason to Go On

ignore others. Encouragement is readily given to the top third or fourth of the class, while students in the bottom half receive the least attention and support.

In discussions and question/answer sessions, teachers usually look more often to the top students. When one of these students misses a question, the teacher assumes the question was unclear and usually rephrases it, giving the student another chance. When a slower student misses a question, the teacher often assumes the question was clear but the learner doesn't know, so the same question is asked of another student. What does this communicate to the class?

Teachers must concentrate on making sure all students are being encouraged, not just a select few.

Slower students especially may need additional encouragement. This may take the form of simply being interested enough to spend some extra time with the student, talking over how he's doing. The extra attention is all the encouragement that many students need.

In the early years, teachers can make effective use of their own approval or disapproval of the child's learning. Generally, young children want to have their teacher's approval, and that can be received in many forms—simple recognition, close physical proximity (being able to sit on the teacher's lap, for instance), gestures, or facial expressions.

Food, awards, and honors are also powerful encouragers when used appropriately. Some reinforcers may be related to primary drives (food, warmth, rest), but most are learned. These include social acceptance and approval by the teacher, parents, and peers. Or they may include objects in some way related to social approval—such as stars or points.

One teacher of junior highers was having trouble keeping them interested in the lesson until he announced that he would be giving quizzes at the end of each class, and

HOW CHILDREN LEARN

anyone who scored 100 on all the tests for the next six weeks would be able to go on a weekend camp-out. That simple encouragement inspired the group to learn—they even helped one another during class so that all of them could go.

Sometimes, however, more is required. Not all students are motivated by the same encouragements. Individualized help is sometimes the only way a child can grasp what he needs to learn. More time on task is required for the child to catch up and keep up. And this is where the teacher needs help.

PARENTS AND OTHER ALLIES

Encouragement is really a very simple process. It is merely paying attention and noticing when someone does something right. But for some reason, that doesn't come naturally. We tend to notice only when something is wrong. The key to effective encouragement is noticing when a person does something right and pointing it out to him.

The three most powerful reinforcers are familiar but often forgotten.
- Attention
- Approval
- Affection

As one veteran teacher said, "Catch them while they're good." That's the key to positive reinforcement. Children tend to think that the only time adults see them is when they're bad. Surprise them! Pay attention and catch them doing something you like. Let them know you approve; do it with affection, if possible, and you will be providing a strong, positive reinforcement.

Because Sunday school teachers aren't able to spend large amounts of time with students, this is where the help of parents is vital. Only with help from the home can enough

A Reason to Go On

time on task be achieved to master the lessons.

Deuteronomy 6: 4-8, part of the famous *Shema* that pious Jews repeat twice daily, says, "Hear, O Israel: The Lord our God, the Lord is one. Love the Lord your God with all your heart and with all your soul and with all your strength. These commandments that I give you today are to be upon your hearts. Impress them on your children. Talk about them when you sit at home and when you walk along the road, when you lie down and when you get up. Tie them as symbols on your hands and bind them on the doorframes of your houses."

Learning, especially spiritual learning, is far more than a classroom affair. Spiritual lessons are meant to be lived in daily activities. And that means the home must play a prominent role.

Parents share the responsibility for teaching their children God's ways, and we must develop a better division of labor between the church and the home. Sunday school teachers can't monitor the progress of individual children the way that parents can, and parents need the help of teachers and the church in giving appropriate instruction.

Parents can be among the best encouragers. The atmosphere established in the home can solidify the learning gained at church, or it can undo it. Teachers and parents need to communicate and let one another know what they are working on with the young people, so that both parents and teachers can be looking for those things and encourage them when they see them.

What about children who don't have Christian parents? This is where other allies come in. Adult "pals" can be informally assigned to these children to spend extra time with them and reinforce the learning. Groups of students can get together to work on specific assignments.

With the encouragement of teachers, parents, and peers, the learning process will be helped immensely.

HOW CHILDREN LEARN

STUDENTS THEMSELVES

Perhaps the strongest encouragement, however, is if the student can see progress in himself. This was what made the difference for Stan in the story at the beginning of this chapter. He had been given the right information—he knew what he was to do—he was making a token effort to do it. But when he saw that he could make progress, suddenly he began to learn. Spelling one more word correctly each week was the ultimate reinforcement. Stan knew he was moving ahead.

Watch a baby who is trying to talk. He or she will work and work and work at it. The child is obsessed with learning. Or watch a young child on the verge of walking. There is a single-minded determination to keep trying until it's accomplished. Why? Because the child knows what the goal is, he's acting to achieve it, and he sees his own progress, step by step.

Learning and spiritual growth come the same way. The best encouragement is seeing your own life improving. Sometimes teachers and parents are needed to draw attention to the progress that's being made. Sometimes tests or self-evaluations can let the student realize his own progress. (See the next chapter for more on self-assessment.) Recognizing little successes is a powerful motivator to continue.

Sometimes when the head of an expedition runs out of words, when the climbers are tired and discouraged and not interested in pep talks, the only way to help is to point out how far the group has come.

"Don't look back" may be good advice for sprinters, but for mountain climbers and learners, occasionally it can be an encouraging practice.

THE VIEW FROM HERE
Assessing

    I looked and saw a parked car covered with snow and ice from storms and snowplows and knew that it could never move until winter passed and warm winds melted the encompassing bonds and that then it could be driven away.
    I looked and saw men working with fluid concrete and saw that they were able to shape and direct it and control it and knew that it would be pliable until time passed and chemical bonds formed and then it would harden and become unmoveable.
    I looked and saw the problems of life and knew that some should be left alone and time would solve them but that others should be dealt with quickly or else they would never pass.
    I looked to see which problems were which and saw that I couldn't.

C. Charles Van Ness
Christian Education Trends

HOW CHILDREN LEARN

6

Sometimes it's not easy to tell whether or not we're on the right track. While climbing a mountain, often the peak is out of sight behind a ridge, a rocky overhang, or a stand of trees. We may not be completely lost, but we don't know our exact location or precisely what direction to go next.

What a relief to emerge from unfamiliar territory to some high, open ground where the view is clear. From there everyone is able to see not only how much progress has been made, but also where the summit is and which route looks most accessible.

In the learning process, people have a need for an occasional clear view to see exactly where they are, how far they've come, and what remains to be done.

No matter what the task—whether a child is learning to bake cookies, ride a bicycle, or live the Christian life—the recurring question is "How am I doing?" The question may be spoken or unspoken, but it's there.

Assessing is the stage in the learning process that answers that question. In order to provide an answer, we must have some standards by which to judge the performance, and this returns us to the planning stage. What goals did we have?

The View from Here

What were we trying to work on? Only if those questions were answered can we know how well we have done.

Psychologist Alfred Adler noted that self-respect is the basic ingredient to mental health. And self-respect comes from that "sense of satisfaction resulting from honest achievement based against some task or standard." Thus, knowing the task is crucial to judging the progress.

People tend to learn faster when this assessing is done regularly. Recently a major university ran an experiment to help people cut back on the amount of energy they were using in their homes. One set of homeowners was given a series of suggestions for cutting down energy consumption and asked to implement them. The second group was given the same suggestions, but the university also installed meters so the people could monitor how much energy was actually being used. After a year, the second group averaged 10 to 15 percent less energy used than those without the immediate feedback.

Assessing a child's learning serves a similar function. It's another way of encouraging—by giving attention and approval to his progress and by letting the child see for himself how well he's doing. Assessing also can catch errors shortly after they occur, before they are compounded with later learning errors.

Another important purpose of assessing is confirming to the learner that he has mastered the material. He knows that he knows. And this accomplishment is an incentive for further learning.

WAYS OF ASSESSING

Assessing can be done in a variety of ways. When a tutor is working with a single student—for example, a mother teach-

HOW CHILDREN LEARN

ing her son how to make chili—the assessing is done immediately and automatically. If the right amounts of the ingredients are put in the pot, the mother nods her approval. But if the child starts to pour chocolate milk into the mixture, his mother immediately makes the necessary correction. And if not, the child quickly realizes the mess he's created. Thus, assessing and correctives are constantly taking place in interactions between a tutor and one student. The process is nonformal and immediate, and is likely to produce a relatively rapid rate of learning.

In most learning situations, however, we don't have the luxury of a one-to-one student/teacher ratio. Sunday school classes may range anywhere from two to two hundred students, and under these conditions, assessing is not automatic—it must be structured.

The most common means of assessing is a quiz or test. These can be effective in letting the students see how well they've learned the material and what remains to be learned. Tests and quizzes are more effective in measuring mental knowledge, however, than they are in assessing attitudes or behavior.

Another way of assessing is the subjective view of the teacher or parents. After observing the child, they can evaluate the progress made. These observations may or may not be accurate, depending on the skill of the observer, and suffer the additional drawback of not allowing the student to see for himself how well he is doing. But feedback from an informal, friendly observer can be valuable.

A third way of assessing is by having students make self-evaluations indicating how well they've mastered the material, perhaps by ranking it on a scale of 1 to 6 (even-numbered scales are better than odd-numbered scales because the student can't conveniently pick the exact middle). When students are asked to rank themselves on several different areas—perhaps how well they're doing on telling

The View from Here

the truth, showing kindness, obeying their parents, etc.—they can see more clearly which areas are succeeding and which need the most work. Then the teacher and parents can focus their efforts there. This method of assessing, of course, is susceptible because it's based solely on the student's perspective.

A combination of the last two means of assessing may be the most appropriate way to gauge progress in attitudes and behaviors. Have both students and teachers fill out evaluations and discuss what needs to be done. Obviously, this works better the older the students are. For younger children, sensitive teachers must stay in tune with the progress and needs of the students.

As Christians mature, the Holy Spirit becomes one of their best sources of assessment. He approves, reproves, convicts, and convinces.

One Christian man said, "I kept wondering how well I was doing in developing loving attitudes. And then I came across a little test in C. S. Lewis's book *Christian Behavior*. He said that love is 'wishing the best for another person,' and the test he gave was imagining that person A told you that something bad had happened to person B, and then the next day you found out it wasn't true. Quick now, were you relieved, or secretly disappointed? That initial attitude determines whether or not you really loved B.

"That little acid test has really helped me work on my love for others. Now I have a way to test it."

Little "acid tests" such as this one can be a valuable source of assessment as well as the means the Holy Spirit uses to help our growth.

Assessing should answer the questions "Where are we succeeding?" and "Where do we need more work?" When tests, observation, or other assessing methods indicate that corrections need to be made, the teacher must determine what adjustments those should be. Generally those adjust-

HOW CHILDREN LEARN

ments fall into one of the following four categories:
- alternative ways of informing.
- additional or alternative ways of practicing.
- additional or alternative means of encouragement.
- some combination of the above.

And with this, the learning process comes full circle. Assessing leads back to one of the earlier stages of informing, doing, and encouraging, and the cycle repeats and continues to be repeated until everything has been learned.

And when our subject is God Himself, that may take a while.

PUTTING IT ALL TOGETHER

Summary and Conclusions

All beginnings are hard.
I can remember hearing my mother murmur those words while I lay in bed with fever. "Children are often sick, darling. That's the way it is with children. All beginnings are hard. You'll be all right soon. . . ."
The man who later guided me in my studies would say to me in his gentle voice, "Be patient. . . . All beginnings are hard. You cannot swallow the world at one time."
I say it to myself today when I stand before a new class at the beginning of a school year . . . All beginnings are hard.
Chaim Potok
In the Beginning

HOW CHILDREN LEARN

7

After reading the ideas in this book, you may be saying, "It's a nice theory, but will it work?"

It may not work . . . perfectly. Nothing does. But a theory does give us something to work toward and helps us anticipate possible results. Even a few steps toward helping children learn better is worth the effort if it helps bring about spiritual growth.

Where do you start? Here are four specific steps to get things moving.

- *Review the steps in the learning process, and consider what adjustments should be made in present teaching methods.*

Here's a brief synopsis; earlier chapters explain in more detail.

Christian education is a means of training children to love God, to obey His commands, and to develop Christian values. This learning process has five phases. As you review these steps, mentally rank how well you are currently putting each of them into practice.

Planning is determining what needs to be learned, how to break it down into manageable portions, and what will be

Putting It All Together

the means of deciding when a child has mastered that bit of learning. Planning is usually done by the curriculum developer, and the church or teacher should adapt those plans to meet their own particular needs.

Informing is letting the student know what needs to be done. Normally a student should be directed to work on one thing at a time, and informing provides the knowledge he needs to succeed. This is the job of the teacher.

Doing is the student's responsibility. The teacher must let him know what to do, but the student must actively be involved, either physically or mentally. For truly life-changing learning, doing must also extend beyond the in-class time. Parents also become involved in this additional "time on task."

Encouraging is done by teachers and, more importantly, by parents. When students make progress, even if it's a small step, parents should notice and reinforce. Attention, approval, and affection are the most powerful ways to make a lesson stick.

Assessing is determining how well the lessons were learned and what needs to be worked on next. This should primarily be the responsibility of the church. While parents know their children deeply, they may not be able to see how they compare with other children their age. Church workers see a larger cross section of students and, by various assessing methods, can determine what has been and what remains to be done.

After mentally ranking your use of these steps, how well did you rate? Where was your strength? How can you improve the one that ranked the lowest?

- *Begin using the ideas described in this book, especially in the younger age levels and each transition year.*

Dr. Benjamin Bloom's research discovered that with traditional teaching techniques, learning differences among children *increased* as time went by. With his "mastery"

HOW CHILDREN LEARN

techniques, and with additional time and encouragement given to the slower learners, Bloom found that learning differences *decreased*—the "slower" learners soon caught up with the faster learners.

Students who have had success early in their learning experience tend to succeed to the same high level in following courses with less and less extra help required. As students "learn to learn," they become better motivated and better prepared for later lessons.

It has also been discovered that students are prepared to learn in a new way at each new school level—elementary, junior high, and senior high. They tend to believe that a new school situation gives them a chance to start afresh, no matter how poorly they did before.

Therefore, the ideas in this book are most powerful at any new beginning, in the early years and at the beginning of junior high and senior high.

• *Meet at least once each quarter with the parents of the students.*

Parents play a vital role in the learning process. They can suggest needs that they see in their children, and if they are to be effective encouragers, they need to know what the teachers will be informing their students and what the students will be trying to do at home. If the parents know what's happening in the Sunday school, they can be watching for ways that their children are living out those lessons and can reinforce them.

The church cannot replace the home as the center of learning, but it can become a coordinating agency between the Sunday school and the home. If this is to be done, the church must take the initiative.

• *Finally, don't give up on anyone.*

Don't write off a student simply because he or she hasn't learned up until now. Maybe alternate ways of informing need to be tried. Maybe additional time or encouragement

Putting It All Together

are necessary. Remember that 95 percent of all children can learn if they are adequately prepared for the new content, if they are well motivated, and if the appropriate learning conditions are provided. Work to provide these conditions. With them, we won't always succeed, but 95 percent isn't a bad average.

Jesus Christ did not intend for His church to be run only by experts, by specialists, by professional consultants. He knew that His church would be filled by reasonably informed lay people who do their best to carry on Christ's ministry.

That's why this book has been written—to help equip reasonably informed people with the tools they need for one particular ministry of the church: to help children learn.

Spiritual learning is like climbing a mountain—God's mountain. It may take an entire lifetime, but it can be scaled. And the view from the top is fantastic.

18357

BV 1475.2 H42

Heck, Glenn.

How children learn

DATE			
MAR 10 '83			
NOV 20 '84			
MAY 17 '85			
MAR 20 '86			
JUL 30 '87			
DE 12 '97			
MY 05 '00			

HIEBERT LIBRARY
Pacific College - M. B. Seminary
Fresno, Calif. 93702

© THE BAKER & TAYLOR CO.